Keeping Your ... Through Diet

True Information About The Negative Effects Of Grain on your Brain

Table of Contents

Introduction

Chapter 1 - The Concept of "Grain Brain"

Chapter 2 - What Do Carbs And Proteins Do To Your Brain And Body?

Chapter 3 - What Does Gluten Do To Your Brain And Body?

Chapter 4 - Paleo Diet and "Grain Brain"

Chapter 5 - Important Health Tests

Chapter 6 - Sample Month Long Grain-Free Meal Plan

Conclusion

Introduction

I want to thank you and congratulate you for downloading the book, "Keeping Your Brain Sharp Through Diet: True Information About the Negative Effects of Grain on Your Brain".

This book contains proven steps and strategies on how to adopt a grain-free lifestyle, and what it means to live grain-free.

If you are having trouble focusing or feel that you might be headed down a dark path toward a future with dementia or some other significant brain disorder, then a grain-free diet is sure to help. Even if you suffer from depression and anxiety, or if you have ADHD, epilepsy, or any number of other brain issues, this book is for you! In this book, you are sure to find many answers to the questions you have always asked about your mental health. You will be able to understand exactly what you need to do in order to change your life for the better and improve the over health of your brain (and body!).

Thanks again for downloading this book, I hope you enjoy it!

Chapter 1 - The Concept of "Grain Brain"

There are many reasons why someone's body might go into decline. For example, those who grow old are more likely to encounter health problems the longer they live. Older bodies simply do not have the tenacity and capability to fight off unwanted disease and bacteria like younger bodies do. Cancer is a major threat to those who are advanced in age, but even simpler diseases such as pneumonia can cause serious problems for those who are unable to fight them off any longer.

Aside from physical health problems, though, more and more people are beginning to suffer from brain issues as they grow older as well. Some older people do not have serious brain deficiencies, and may be able to laugh them off as just having a "senior brain." But others may have much more severe problems, including Alzheimer's disease. These kinds of illnesses are no joking matter, and they affect thousands of people every single day. Dementia and its related illnesses can keep people from being able to access their stored memories or form any new ones, and it can also interfere so severely with daily life that those who fall victim to it can no longer care for themselves. Many people fear this outcome. It can be truly a fate worse than death.

You may have heard that Alzheimer's is an inevitable part of growing older. You may believe that since one of your blood relatives suffered from Alzheimer's disease, that you are destined to do the same. But these traditional beliefs about Alzheimer's and other forms of dementia may not be exactly true. There are many ways in which you can help your brain and take care of it, ensuring that you will not have to face the threat of Alzheimer's when you are older. And if you are already in the age range for dementia, don't worry! It's never too late to begin working on the health of your brain.

Alzheimer's isn't the only disorder you can fight, however. Depression, fatigue, migraines, epilepsy, and anxiety are all brain dysfunctions that you are absolutely able to combat, given that you are armed with the proper weapons. And what are those weapons? A healthy diet and exercise, of course!

You've probably been told throughout your whole life that a healthy diet and exercise are the ways to lose weight and stay in shape. And this is definitely very true! Eating well is a great way to balance out the amount of good and bad food groups you consume in a day. Following a prescribed diet plan can help you to avoid eating too many of one type of food, such as carbohydrates, fats, or calories, and can help you focus on eating those kinds of foods that are much better for you, such as proteins, vitamins, and omega-3 fatty acids. Many different types of diet plans are great options for weight loss, and several of those plans can be combined with each other to create the perfect diet for you and your lifestyle. Everyone is different, so one diet that works for someone you know may not work as well for you. It is important to experiment with diet plans and find the ones that are right for you.

If you couple your dieting with regular exercise, you are sure to reap even more physical rewards for your hard work! You will feel great and be fit and in shape in no time if you combine a healthy diet with exercise. Exercising regularly can help you to lower your heart rate and cholesterol, increase muscle mass in your body, and improve your hear and lung capabilities. You can even keep joint pain under control through exercise.

Obviously, diet and exercise do a lot for your physical well-being. But what about your mental health? There is so much more diet and exercise can accomplish for you in the realm of your brain! Eating a healthy diet and maintaining your exercise schedule can help you keep focused and can even improve the physical health of your brain, as well. But what kind of diet is the best kind for brain health?

It may come as a surprise to you, but the best diet for your brain is a diet that does not include grain. That's right—grains are terrible for your mental health. This statement definitely does include bleached, heavily processed grains that can be found in white bread, white rice, and white noodles. However, it goes far beyond that. It also includes the whole wheats that many people believe are extra healthy and good for our bodies. Even multigrain breads and the like are no good for your brain. Basically, if it contains a grain, it does not need to be in your body.

You may be unwilling to accept this concept. You may think back to all the times you have been told, perhaps even by your doctor, that you should eat nothing but whole wheat items in order to help with your weight loss and dietary goals. And you may be thinking that a grain-free diet surely must just be some kind of a fad. It's understandable that you might have trouble with the idea of cutting grains completely out of your diet; in a modern world, it is next to impossible to avoid eating way too many servings of grains on a daily basis. As a matter of fact, we have all been told for so long that we need grains, that it is difficult to imagine some meals without them. Where would your soup be without crackers? Where would your dip be without bread?

But calm down! It is actually very easy to adapt your lifestyle into a grain-free one. There are plenty of substitutes that can take the place of your favorite grainy foods with no problem. And you will be okay if you have to eat soup without crackers! Remember, for every food you give up on this diet, you are gaining so much more health for your brain. You will be giving your brain the ability to repair itself, to fight off mental illness, to stay focused all day long, and to keep your body alive and well for a long time to come.

If you feel like you may have already suffered irreversible damage to your brain from your past diet, again, fear not. A healthy diet is still going to help you significantly. Your brain has a fantastic ability called neuroplasticity that ensures that it can reorganize itself, change, and shift to accommodate any problems it may encounter. If you have suffered some damage to your brain, the neuroplasticity of your most important organ is going to help you work around it. You only need to provide it a healthy environment in which to do so. And once again, that is where a healthy diet comes in to play!

Chapter 2 - What Do Carbs And Proteins Do To Your Brain And Body?

Carbohydrates are one of the three main types of food that our body digests on a daily basis. The other types are proteins and fats. The body needs proteins and fats in the diet every single day, but we do not technically need any carbohydrates. Many low-carb diets tout the need to eat a few carbs a day, usually limiting them to 50 grams or fewer. However, if your body can handle a complete lack of carbs in your daily diet, there is absolutely no need to eat them at all.

It is true that there are some "good carbs" out there in the dietary world. These are usually carbs that can be easily metabolized and come from healthy sources, such as potatoes. However, it is once again not necessary to consume these "good carbs" at all, and it remains best to avoid them no matter what.

When you are trying to lose weight, carbohydrates are only a hindrance. You can sometimes have success watching your weight with other dietary limitations, such as fat or calories, but limiting your carbs is the best way to lose weight quickly and keep it off for good. Basically, when you eat food, your body uses carbohydrates first to help supply energy to the entire body. This stops the fat from being accessed and burned as an energy source. When you no longer eat carbohydrates, the fat stores in your body will be burned much more quickly, since fat will be the first source your body goes to for energy. You will also need to eat much more protein to keep up the energy levels in your body and to keep it burning fat as much as possible. This is great, because protein is very, very good for you!

So, in short, eating few to no carbs every day and packing your diet with protein is a great way to lose weight and stay in shape. And if you do just the opposite—if you eat way too many carbohydrates and don't supplement your diet with lots of protein—you are never going to be able to shed the pounds you hope to get rid of. You will feel bloated and lethargic, and probably won't even have the energy to get up and exercise. All in all, eating carbs is no good for your body.

And carbs are even worse for your brain! When you eat carbs, your brain becomes fogged and confused, and you may have trouble focusing on your work. You may get depressed from the inflammation in your brain that is caused by the over-consumption of carbohydrates, and you may not even feel like partaking in the hobbies you used to enjoy anymore. Eating too many carbs can have a severe effect on your life, mentally as well as physically.

You might be concerned that the over-abundance of meat in your diet could lead to problems, as well. In some ways, you are right to have those concerns. Red meat in particular is almost always grain-fed and therefore can cause you to consume grains whether you want to or not! Because of this, it is vitally important to always consume red meat that has been grass-fed rather than grain-fed. The same is true of fowl. Your poultry meat should come from pasture-raised chickens and turkeys that have not been force-fed grains. You should also strive to eat truly cage-free eggs that come from chickens that have been allowed to eat a natural diet rather than grains.

Chapter 3 -What Does Gluten Do To Your Brain And Body?

About two percent of the population suffers from celiac disease, which is a severe allergic reaction to gluten in any form. Even the tiniest crumb of a gluten-filled food item can set off an allergic reaction in these people. But, you may be thinking, not everyone responds that way to gluten, right? So what is it about gluten that is so bad?

First of all, no one can completely metabolize gluten. When you digest it, it can and very often does cause damage to your gut. This damage can include a destroyed stomach lining, tears in your gut that can result in ulcers, severe bloating and gas, constipation, unhealthy stool, and inflammation of the digestive system. You may develop chronic digestive issues from the damage to your gut that can take years to repair—and your digestive system may not ever be able to be fully restored to its original capabilities. Regardless of whether or not you have celiac disease, you may be facing any number of other diseases, disorders, and dysfunctions from the ingestion of gluten on a frequent basis.

Even if you do not have celiac disease, roughly one third of the population does have a sensitivity to gluten. A gluten sensitivity causes severe reactions that can range from inflammatory bowel disorders to chronic migraines to inability to lose weight, and more. Gluten sensitivity can even lead to depression, Alzheimer's disease, ADHD, and other mental health disorders. If you are someone who is sensitive to gluten, or if you believe you might be, pay close attention to how it makes you feel after you eat it. If you get bloated, constipated, or have sickly-looking bowel movements shortly after eating gluten, chances are you have a gluten sensitivity. If you have headaches that come on quickly after gluten consumption, or if you feel like your brain is in a fog and you cannot focus after you eat gluten, once again, you may have a gluten sensitivity.

It is not difficult at all, these days, to adopt a gluten-free lifestyle, which is by its very nature a grain-free lifestyle. In the past, it was much more difficult for those who were avoiding gluten to keep it out of their diets. However, nowadays, gluten free foods can be found on the shelves in most supermarkets and grocery stores. Just be wary when you are looking at pre-packaged gluten free foods. In many situations, unfortunate other ingredients have been added to these foods to make them more appetizing or appealing; however, those ingredients can and often do include sources that still contain grain! They also may contain chemicals that are also very unhealthy for your body and your brain. If you are purchasing pre-packaged gluten free foods, be sure to carefully read the ingredients list. Many are perfectly healthy, but it pays to be careful.

Remember that, when you are trying to avoid gluten, the best possible way is to simply cut out forms of food that might have gluten in the first place. For example, you do not need to eat bread or bread products; there are other ways to eat noodles without consuming pasta; and desserts can be delicious without any flour involved! The best way to enjoy a healthy and grain-free diet is to simply eat meat, fruit, and vegetables. These food groups never contain a trace of gluten!

Also remember that, if you have celiac disease or a very high sensitivity to gluten, packaged foods can be labeled "gluten free" in the United States if they still contain trace amounts of gluten. So, if they are made on the same machinery that processes foods with gluten in them, they can still be called gluten free. This does not bear any significance for those who are trying to avoid gluten for a normal degree of sensitivity, or for those who are trying to keep their "grain brain" away. However, it is worth noting for those who might have a terrible reaction even from one crumb of gluten. When in doubt, read the labels!

Chapter 4 - Paleo Diet and "Grain Brain"

The paleo diet and lifestyle is also known as the paleolithic lifestyle, and it has been increasing in popularity for the past few years since it was introduced. You have likely heard of the paleo lifestyle and diet, but you may not have a full understanding of what it includes. You probably did not even realize that a paleo diet can and does work perfectly with a grain-free lifestyle—and that is what this chapter is here to explain!

A paleo diet begins with the concept of eating "like a caveman would." This is the building block of everything paleo. When you imagine cavemen, or, more accurately, the early hunter-gatherers, what do you think of them eating? Do you imagine them coming back from a long day of hunting with perhaps a deer carcass to serve for a meal? Do you picture the women going out and finding berries, roots, and other edible plants that they might have enjoyed with the deer? If so, you're pretty much on the right track. Early hunter-gatherers would have hunted their prey and served the meat after roasting it over a flame. They would have happily enjoyed plants that they found growing wild, and later in human history, they might have grown those plants themselves to cultivate for eating and for medicinal purposes, too. Human beings have progressed to an age in which we purchase our food from the market and no longer have to go out and attack our nightly dinners. This is all well and good, but there was definitely something to the way of life of the early primitive people!

The paleo diet works so well on a grain-free diet because, at its core, a paleo diet completely removes the ingestion of grains. Human bodies simply were not built to successfully metabolize the gluten and carbohydrates found in grains. Because of this, we suffer considerably more as a species with inflammation of the gut and other problems with the digestive system—not to mention with those brain disorders we all want to desperately to fight—than primitive people did. Early hunter-gatherers simply would not have had the knowledge to plant, grow, process, or cook with grains, so they would not have eaten them. When following a paleo diet, it is very necessary to remember that grains are not to be consumed. Therefore, this makes the paleo diet and lifestyle excellent candidates for helping you on your grain-free journey to rid yourself of "grain brain!"

Aside from grains, sugar must also be excluded form a paleo style diet. Early hunter-gatherers would not have consumed sugar on a regular basis. They would, however, have obtained sugars naturally through fruits and honey. They likely ate a great deal of fruits in their natural state, and probably consumed both honey and the comb frequently. Therefore, when following a paleo diet, you can eat fruit and can sweeten your foods with honey as much as you like. This also bodes well for a grain-free diet and for helping your brain's health to improve. Cutting back on sugars helps to cut back on carbohydrates, and can keep you from developing diabetes, too.

Dairy is an iffy point when it comes to paleo dieting. Some paleo lifestyle followers believe that dairy and eggs should never be consumed. However, it is impossible to believe that early hunter-gatherers would never have consumed dairy and eggs. They likely would have had eggs from many different sources, including less common ones in our modern day society (such as snake eggs and similar). Dairy may have been more difficult for them to find, but it is still highly probable that they consumed it under some circumstances. For the purposes of a successful diet to rid yourself of "grain brain" and keep your body and brain healthy and happy, you should still consume dairy and eggs. They are excellent sources of calcium and protein, both of which you need. However, dairy should be consumed in smaller amounts, due to the high concentration of fats.

To make a long story short, the paleo diet works amazingly well as a diet plan and lifestyle that can help you get your brain health under control. It focuses on eating what early hunter-gatherers would have eaten, which includes anything they could find, pick, grow, or hunt. A paleo diet never includes grains or sugar, but can include honey as a sweetener. There are endless possibilities to what you can enjoy when you follow this type of diet, so give it a try—it it sure to help you fight your "grain brain" successfully!

Chapter 5 - Important Health Tests

Whether you have just started a journey toward weight loss, getting fit, and improving the overall health of your body and brain, or you have been working toward these goals for some time already and you plan to switch to a grain-free method of dieting, there are several medical tests which you should consider having performed at your earliest convenience. Most insurance plans cover these tests, and they are already quite affordable, widely-available forms of lab work. The best reason to have these tests performed is to get an idea of how badly at risk you are for brain disease and degeneration in the future. They can also show you where you on the path toward brain health right now, and may even help you catch any budding problems before they get too serious. Ask your doctor for these lab tests next time you visit.

Hemoglobin A1C Test - This is a blood test that helps you get an understanding for your average blood sugar levels over a 90-day period. Through this test, you can tell how well you are controlling your blood sugar levels overall. This test also allows you to see any damage that has occurred to your brain's proteins due to your blood sugar levels. In this way, you can easily see if your brain is suffering damage over time.

Fasting Blood Glucose Test - This test helps you find out if you are diabetic or pre-diabetic. First, you must not eat for 8 hours; then, the doctor (or lab technician) will draw blood to check the amount of sugar (or glucose) in your blood. If the results come back anywhere between 70 and 100 milligrams per deciliter, you are in the "normal" range. If they are higher than this, you may have some insulin problems that could lead toward diabetes and brain damage. If the numbers are lower than this, it could still be a sign that you may be on the path to diabetes.

Fasting Insulin Test - This blood test shows any increases in the levels of insulin in your body. If insulin levels rise, this indicates that your pancreas is working too hard, due to too many carbohydrates in your diet. Insulin levels that stay too high for too long can not only lead to diabetes, but also lead to inflammation of the brain and brain disorders. This test works well as an early warning of diabetes.

Fructosamine Test - A fructosamine test works similarly to the way a Hemoglobin A1C Test works. It also measures your blood sugar levels over a period of time, but this time is shorter, at about two weeks. This can still be an effective way to test your blood sugar levels, but may not provide as full of a picture as the Hemoglobin test will.

Vitamin D Test - This blood test will help see the levels of Vitamin D in your brain. Vitamin D is a steroid hormone found in the brain that can help keep inflammation levels low. A normal level of Vitamin D in the brain can help you fight Alzheimer's, epilepsy, Parkinson's disease, and even schizophrenia.

Homocysteine Test - Homocysteine is an amino acid that the body produces. When there is too much of this amino acid in the body, you may be at a higher risk for hardened arteries, stroke and heart attack, heart disease, and dementia.

C-reactive Protein Test - These proteins, in high numbers, indicate significant inflammation in the brain and body. Testing for them can help you find out early on if there is a problem, and try to locate the source of the issue.

Cyrex Array 3 and Cyrex Array 4 Tests - A Cyrex Array 3 Test signifies whether or not you are allergic to gluten; it is the best test available for gluten sensitivity and celiac disease. The Cyrex Array 4 Test is similar to the 3, but also tests for twenty-four other foods that you may be sensitive to if you have a problem with gluten.

Remember that these tests are very important and can help you figure out where you stand in the realm of body and brain health. However, if you cannot afford to have them performed right away, do not let that stop you from beginning a grain-free diet today!

Chapter 6 - Sample Month Long Grain-Free Meal Plan

Monday

breakfast - Fruit smoothie

lunch - Tuna salad lettuce wrap

dinner - Ginger orange chicken

Tuesday

breakfast - Quinoa hot cereal

lunch - Mason jar salad

dinner - Burger patties on a salad

Wednesday

breakfast - Fruit smoothie

lunch - Tuna salad lettuce wrap

dinner - Slow cooker chicken wings

Thursday

breakfast - Quinoa hot cereal

lunch - Mason jar salad

dinner - Salmon stir fry with Asian vegetables

Friday

breakfast - Fruit smoothie

lunch - Tuna salad lettuce wrap

dinner - Breakfast for dinner (eggs, bacon or sausage, fruit, cheese)

Saturday

breakfast - Pancakes made with coconut "flour"

lunch - Beef stew

dinner - Sloppy Joes on a salad

Sunday

breakfast - Fried mushrooms with poached eggs

lunch - Beef stew

dinner - Dill salmon and asparagus

Monday

breakfast - Boiled eggs and fried bacon

lunch - Chicken salad lettuce wrap

dinner - Peach glazed chicken

Tuesday

breakfast - Fruit smoothie

lunch - Mason jar salad

dinner - Salmon patties on a salad

Wednesday

breakfast - Boiled eggs and fried bacon

lunch - Chicken salad lettuce wrap

dinner - Roast turkey with apple stuffing

Thursday

breakfast - Fruit smoothie

lunch - Mason jar salad

dinner - Citrus-topped salmon with cucumber salad

Friday

breakfast - Boiled eggs and fried bacon

lunch - Chicken salad lettuce wrap

dinner - Pork chops and steamed green beans

Saturday

breakfast - Huevos Rancheros

lunch - Homemade tomato soup

dinner - Taco salad (no shell)

Sunday

breakfast - Crepes made with coconut "flour"

lunch - Homemade tomato soup

dinner - Herbed salmon and asparagus

Monday

breakfast - Quinoa porridge

lunch - Bean salad lettuce wrap

dinner - Shrimp cakes on salad

Tuesday

breakfast - Fruit smoothie

lunch - Carrot soup in a mason jar

dinner - Lemon pepper chicken

Wednesday

breakfast - Quinoa porridge

lunch - Bean salad lettuce wrap

dinner - Sausage and peppers

Thursday

breakfast - Fruit smoothie

lunch - Carrot soup in a mason jar

dinner - Salmon with tomato relish

Friday

breakfast - Quinoa porridge

lunch - Bean salad lettuce wrap

dinner - Chicken parmesan

Saturday

breakfast - Scones made with coconut "flour"

lunch - Asparagus salad with basil

dinner - Shrimp scampi

Sunday

breakfast - Fried eggs with sausage gravy (use almond flour in gravy)

lunch - Beet salad with carrot

dinner - Mango glazed chicken

Monday

breakfast - Fruit smoothie

lunch - Salmon salad lettuce wrap

dinner - Grilled tilapia with asparagus

Tuesday

breakfast - Cantaloupe with almond milk

lunch - Mason jar salad

dinner - Chili lime chicken

Wednesday

breakfast - Fruit smoothie

lunch - Salmon salad lettuce wrap

dinner - Ratatouille

Thursday

breakfast - Cantaloupe with almond milk

lunch - Mason jar salad

dinner - Shrimp curry

Friday

breakfast - Fruit smoothie

lunch - Salmon salad lettuce wrap

dinner - Breakfast for dinner (eggs, bacon or sausage, fruit, cheese)

Saturday

breakfast - Pumpkin muffins made with coconut "flour"

lunch - Cauliflower soup in a mason jar

dinner - Meatballs on a salad

Sunday

breakfast - Stir-fry veggies with poached eggs

lunch - Cauliflower soup in a mason jar

dinner - Roast chicken with broccoli

Conclusion

Thank you again for downloading this book!

I hope this book was able to help you to fully understand the concept of "grain brain" and how it can affect your life. By now, you should be able to adopt this lifestyle and use it to help benefit your brain and body both. The path to a grain-free life may not always be easy, but your brain will thank you for following it.

The next step is to cut out those grains and get ready to enjoy a clearer, more focused, and healthier brain!

Printed in Great Britain
by Amazon